Lilias Yoga and You

This book is as relaxed and happy as the happy art of relaxation it teaches you. As Lilias, its graceful author, says, "Everything about Yoga is natural—nothing is *forced* on you." You adapt Yoga to *your* lifestyle, developing your *own* inner qualities of serenity and balance.

Why not start today? What you put into these exercises you will get back, doubled. And it may be one of the great adventures—physical, mental and spiritual—of your life.

About the Author

LILIAS FOLAN lives in Cincinnati with her husband and two young sons. Her television program, which first appeared as a local show on WCET in Cincinnati, is now syndicated and appears on more than 193 educational television stations.

Lilias Yoga and You

By Lilias M. Folan

BANTAM BOOKS
TORONTO · NEW YORK · LONDON · SYDNEY

DEDICATED TO

My husband, Bob.
whose love and patience are my guideposts on the
path.
Sri Swami Chidananda Maharaj
Sri Swami Pranananda
Dr. Paul Worthen Dale
Hans and Sita Frenkel
Ida Grylla
Char and the Scattered Brotherhood

*This low-priced Bantam Book
has been completely reset in a type face
designed for easy reading, and was printed
from new plates. It contains the complete
text of the original hard-cover edition.*
NOT ONE WORD HAS BEEN OMITTED

RL 8, IL 8-up

LILIAS YOGA AND YOU

A Bantam Book / published by arrangement with
WCET-TV

PRINTING HISTORY
WCET-TV edition / April 1972
2nd edition / December 1972   5th edition / December 1973
3rd edition / April 1973   6th edition / May 1974
4th edition / June 1973   7th edition / January 1975
8th edition / August 1975

Bantam edition / February 1976
7 printings through July 1980

ISBN 0-553-14390-5

Published simultaneously in the United States and Canada

PRINTED IN THE UNITED STATES OF AMERICA

16 15 14 13 12 11 10 9 8

Contents

Lilias Yoga and You

Slow Me Down, Lord

Slow me down, Lord! Ease the pounding of my heart by the quieting of my mind. Steady my hurried pace with a vision of the eternal reach of time.

Give me, amidst the confusion of my day, the calmness of the everlasting hills. Break the tensions of my nerves and muscles with the music of the singing streams that live in my memory.

Help me to know the magic restoring power of sleep.

Teach me the art of taking Minute Vacations . . . of slowing down to look at a flower, to chat with a friend, to pat a dog, to read a few lines from a good book.

Remind me each day of the fable of the hare and the tortoise that I may know that the race is not always to the swift; that there is more to life than increasing its speed.

Let me look upward into the branches of the towering oak and know that it grew great and strong because it grew slowly and well. Slow me down, Lord, and inspire me to send my roots deep into the soil of life's enduring values that I may grow toward the stars of my greater destiny.   Amen.

—WILFRED A. PETERSON

Wilfred A. Peterson in Adventures in the Art of Living, *published by Simon and Schuster, New York.*

Introduction

I sit here at my desk pondering how best to start the little book I want to write especially for you. Many illuminating books have been written about Hatha Yoga. This book is not written to join this vast and ever-growing collection. It comes out as my answer to the many letters and questions you have sent to me as a Yoga teacher during the past nine years. Pictures flash through my mind. I see you as the businessman, the housewife, the grandmother and the student. All making up one glorious class! I long to know each one of you personally. Perhaps one day I will have that pleasure.

Little new can be written about Hatha Yoga. It was all put down beautifully long ago by the great ancient teachers. My only longing is to share with you some of what Hatha Yoga and Yoga Philosophy has given to me. To share with you some of my inner thoughts, feelings and experiences. Take what you think is interesting. Put it into your life and disregard all that you do not find applicable. This is my simple offering of thoughts, questions and answers for beginners.

Random Thoughts

I could spend a great deal of time using many Sanskrit words to explain the principles of Yoga. But those words mean little, unless they are put to use. What does mean something? Your own personal experience means something not from a book, nor a lecture. This is what you can expect from Hatha Yoga. Your own personal experience, especially designed for you and your life style.

Yoga means union. Union with what, you ask? Union with all that you are. All that is your heritage. All that is your potential—total union in experience: physical, mental and spiritual.

We spend years in high schools and colleges to learn about the outer things. Billions of dollars are spent going to the moon learning about celestial things. But, how much do we really know about our inner universe?

Hundreds of years ago, Patanjali, a great man of wisdom, formulated a scientific system of spiritual exercises. It was especially for the esoteric, the totally committed, with an unquenchable thirst for God. To know God was not attained in a day. So, to begin with the basic instruments, the body and mind were made fit and healthy for that great task. It was difficult to search for God if the body was full of aches, pains and stiffness and the mind ridden with erratic thoughts and desires.

The ancient men of wisdom evolved this scientific system of exercises called Hatha Yoga to promote a physical fitness and mental well being.

Here we are in the 1970's. Many still search for God. We are all in different phases of our lives. Family life, business problems, school responsibilities, everyday living, take our energies. Many long for the simple gift of a restful night's sleep without resorting to pills. Others yearn to fit into the size dress or suit that has been hanging unused in their closet. For some, to go into the evening hours full of energy or waken with optimism would be a gift, and for still others, to approach their sixties with confidence, vigor and balance. All needs are important! You are important.

As you proceed with your Yoga studies, watch yourself go from strength to strength. Please keep a notebook and write down all that is discouraging as well as encouraging. Be attentive to what you feel, what you sense, especially in the beginning. (My first notebook has my old unwanted weight, 145, written in it.) It will be fun to look back and see where you have been. This helps you understand where you are going. I have included blank pages in the back to start your Hatha Yoga notebook. Start today!

Armed with curiosity and expectancy, together we embark upon one of the greatest adventures of your life; Hatha Yoga, whether you are 14, 40 or 65. Rejoice! This is the beginning.

Thoughts on Beauty

If you want a beautiful or handsome body, you will have it with Hatha Yoga. What you put into these exercises you will get back, doubled! There are some excellent non-Yoga books on facial exercises for men and women. But, many lines in the face and a lack of youthful glow will be taken care of as you progress with your Asanas (postures).

I really am "bugged" with fashion magazines that constantly encourage youthfulness, for men and women, as a goal in life. How absurd! I feel it is extremely important to prepare through exercises, diet and proper outlook for our forties, fifties, sixties and seventies, developing qualities within that will give us contentment and balance.

My teacher, Swami Chidananda, said this to me and I share it with you: "You know, Gandhi was not very beautiful, but millions were attracted to him, and why? Because he had qualities. Jesus Christ was not a cinema actor. Although they paint Him to be very beautiful, He must have been a very rough and weatherbeaten sort of fellow. He lived most of the time in the open air, and in the Middle East there were hot sun and dry winds. And yet, you see, He was attractive to men, women and children, learned and ignorant. All were attracted because there was something about Him and, also, His qualities . . . . His kindness, His compassion, His gentleness and His desire to help others. Cultivate the beauty of your inner nature."

Thinking About Food

I like to think that this body has been given to me as a gift on loan for 80 years or more. That it is going to work at its highest potential, at any age, if I help it by eating the cleanest, healthiest, purest foods and drink.

Everything about Yoga is natural and nothing is forced on you. Perhaps experimenting (with your doctor's permission) with a balanced diet of fruits, fresh vegetables, salads, wheat breads and herb teas might be interesting to you.

Whether you are 80 or 18, start where you are now. Take a serious look at your food habits. Perhaps reading something on the matter would be helpful.

Personally, I am not a vitamin pill popper. However, I take a natural multipurpose vitamin each day. I am a label reader and try to pick products with the least preservatives, food coloring and added vitamins.

A diet consisting of fruit in the early morning and mid-morning, a huge salad of fresh vegetables and herbs from my garden for lunch is my aspiration. Also I enjoy yogurt, sprouted beans and avocado (fattening, but high in protein). Then for dinner, a baked yam or potato, and a lightly steamed vegetable, also drinking the steamed vegetable broth and eating more salad. When I give my family red meat, I usually serve them but not myself. Papaya-mint tea with a little honey or raw sugar is delicious after dinner. Yes, I am very unYogic and drink coffee in the morning.

Go to your health food store. There you will find organically grown vegetables, wonderful dried fruits and nuts and, usually, an interesting selection of health foods and cookbooks. But, bring your checkbook. They are expensive! I have found some wonderful organic farms in my area. The soil is rich and black. The vegetables are huge and fresh. The farmer takes such pride and care in his art of growing vegetables organically.

Many of you have written me about your own organic gardens at home. I think this is just great!

Caution: Moderation and balance in all things. This means examining and rearranging your pattern of eating if it is necessary. It also means not getting hung up on health foods or fads. Use your commonsense!

"Are You a Vegetarian?"

Yes, whenever possible. I never had to force myself to become a vegetarian. It happened naturally and spontaneously. It would not occur to me to impose it upon you. All I ask is that you keep your mind open to the subject.

Vegetarian cooking can be creative and interesting. Not only for the cook but for those at the table.

Whether you eat meat or not, approaching your cooking job with care and love makes such a difference. That is what is really important.

10

My Favorite Vegetarian Recipe

Egg and Brown Rice Casserole

1¼ cups brown rice
3 cups water
5 hard boiled eggs, diced
3 tablespoons chopped chives
½ cup chopped pecans
1 cup chopped celery
½ cup chopped black olives
½ cup grated sharp cheddar cheese
½ cup yogurt
1 cup milk
3 tablespoons safflower oil
1 teaspoon (sea) salt
1 teaspoon Accent
1½ cups Rusk (or bread) crumbs
½ stick safflower margarine
1½ teaspoons tarragon leaves

Cover and cook rice in 3 cups of water until tender. Put into a mixing bowl. Add all ingredients except Rusk crumbs and oil. Cut margarine in small pieces. Add tarragon leaves pulverized between your palms. Mix gently and put in lightly oiled casserole. Top with Rusk crumbs which have been moistened with the safflower oil. Bake in moderate oven, 300 degrees, until set and the crumbs are a golden brown. Serves 6 to 8.

(From: "Mike & Olga's Favorite Recipes" by Mike and Olga Teichner, published by the Naylor Company.)

Comments and Questions

What is Observation?

Observation means closing the eyes and using your inner sight (insight) to sense and feel how your body reacts to each posture. Observation, with each posture, is one difference between Hatha Yoga and Trimnastics.

Sense and feel the changes going on externally and internally. Observe the skin, how it begins to tingle and feel warm. Sense the stretching of your muscles as you hold the posture. With the release of the stretch, note warmth and subtle energy flow to areas that have been released from tension and fatigue. Observe how difficult or easy it is for you to suggest to your body to relax deeply for 10 minutes. Write your observation down.

As you proceed with your inner and outer study, you will make "observation" become a useful and healthy tool. You will spot the restlessness of your mind or unconsciously negative thinking. Once you are aware of this happening, replace the negative thought with an uplifting and positive one. It really works! You can use this to strengthen your everyday living.

Positive Mental Suggestion

Have you ever listened to your inner talking or watched "YOU" as an observer observing yourself? Usually we will hear little sentences, "I am cold." "She is pretty." The other day I watched a quizzical, thoughtful look cross my eight-year-old son's face. I asked him what he was thinking. He said, "I was just listening to the voice inside me that is never quiet."

This is what I call inner talking. In moments of relaxation you can observe its restlessness. After a long day at the office, it is hard to turn off. Now I want you to do an exercise with me. Close your eyes. Quietly observe inner talking and restlessness. Carefully sense and feel the mental and physical changes as you read the next words. CANCER! ANGER! PAIN! Continue repeating one of these words. Try to imagine repeating this word for two hours. How would you feel? Restless? Discontented? Sad? Tightened stomach? Fatigue?

The second part of the exercise is:

Close your eyes. Quiet your mind by focusing it on your breath. Now repeat one of these words. JOY! PEACE! SMILE! LOVE! Hold your mind to one of these. Observe the inner mental and physical changes. Continue for several minutes. How do you feel? Uplifted? Peaceful? Happy? Joyous? Energetic? Yes, I'm sure many of you could feel the difference inside yourself as you repeated two opposite words. All are heavy with connotation and association. Some part of us hears and records everything we say outwardly and inwardly. It is stored in the depths of us. Some is remembered. Some is not. But it is there.

Positive suggestion is turning this inner talking to positive, everyday, strong good use! How often we "suggest ourselves" into a bad, dreary mood or into fatigue. "It won't work." "I'm too tired." "I can't possibly do that." Down, down we pull ourselves. Not knowing we are listening with inner ears to all we suggest to ourselves.

Give yourself firm and positive mental suggestions. Such as "I am bringing new energy into my body when I inhale." "As I exhale, out goes all tension and tiredness." "I feel happy." or, "Help is here." Even when you find you do not feel that way, you can reverse the currents. Stop the squirrel caging of the mind with a little self-discipline and THINK-UP.

Of course it will take some time and effort. It is really a matter of catching yourself in an old habit. Please write down your efforts. Make it a game that you can play standing in front of your stove, behind your desk or in a classroom.

"Am I spending too much time thinking about myself?"

All of us have guilty moments when this nagging question runs across our minds. Self-knowledge is not only essential to you but a great aid in your

association with others. Because, to the extent you know yourself you will know your fellowman.

You are important! Not from the huge ego or "I" sense, but as a working part of a family or a living unit in any situation.

Find an hour each day for yourself. (Sometimes, if my schedule is heavy, I arise an hour earlier.) Do a little Hatha Yoga, breathing exercises, meditation or uplifting reading. If one hour is not possible, devote one half hour to yourself alone. Give me one hour to myself and I will give you back twenty-three complete and full ones to help others.

"How long is your own daily practice?"

Each day I take one half hour minimum for asanas (postures) and 10 minutes for breathing and relaxation. Once a week I give myself a good hour-and-a-half workout! The time of day I have chosen (4:30 P.M.) would not be good for everyone. It recharges me for my evening of dinner, children, homework, etc. I also do not feel as hungry and, therefore, eat less. Sleep also comes effortlessly. In the beginning, however, I practiced one hour (sometimes two) each day and participated in two classes a week for two years. I felt so well and was really challenged with the whole Hatha Yoga concept. But for beginners, one half hour a day would be perfect.

"Do You Smoke?"

No. Hurrah! When I first started taking Hatha Yoga classes, I used to smoke a little less than a pack a day. Gradually I noticed that the clean feeling I felt after class would go as soon as I lit up a cigarette.

I never gave the habit up. It gave me up. Yoga breathing was a tremendous help, along with the postures. Perhaps it will not be as quick for you, but I know Hatha Yoga will be helpful if you let it happen!

"Lilias, I feel so enthusiastic about Hatha Yoga I can't wait to get my husband (or wife) into a class."

Dear Friend,

I remember when I ran home after beginning Hatha Yoga at the Y.W.C.A. exclaiming to my wonderful husband that he must join me. Not only that, I vividly recall demonstrating a headstand one evening in the middle of a party. (Much to his horror!) My husband did not want a Hatha Yoga class. He felt just fine, thank you very much!! Now, we both chuckle about it.

But, looking deeper into the situation, I learned two things. One was that the only person you can really change is yourself. Share . . . of course! Yoga is to bring family harmony and peace. Quietly and serenely you can become an example of Hatha Yoga. Your wife (or husband) will notice the change and through your example the family will join you!

About showing off at a party . . . well. All this Yoga business is a private matter. (I remember a friend of mine who was trying a headstand at a party and she rolled into a coffee table which put her out of commission for a few weeks.) Keep your exercises to the privacy of your garden or bedroom. You'll be happier with yourself the next day!

"If I am Pregnant . . ."

How wonderful! First ask your doctor about participation in our class. Better still, ask him to watch our class. Bring along this book. Do what he recommends, please.

Everyone is built differently. If you are a three-year veteran of Hatha Yoga or just starting, go slowly and carefully. If it hurts, stop. Two definitely NOT for the pregnant lady are locust and stomach lift. Breathing exercises will be helpful for energy during pregnancy and during delivery.

Mathew, Lilias and Michael Folan practicing the Lion

"After the Baby"

As soon as the doctor says to exercise, you are ready for almost everything. The shoulder stand will help to bring female organs back into proper position. Stomach lift, to firm and tighten up abdomen.

Do not be discouraged with a little extra weight. Think positively and optimistically. In a few months, with half an hour a day, a little dieting, the body will be better than ever! One of the highlights of last year's class was a sweet girl who had gained 30 pounds during pregnancy. The burden of carrying the weight mentally and physically was heavy. Three months of diet and Yoga exercises restored her figure and calmness, plus energy to care for her husband and baby. Her words to me at the last class before summer vacation were, "I feel like I'm the one who's been born."

"How much time each day should I practice?"

As long as you wish. Each year at our Yoga retreat, I'll spend up to three hours a day on Hatha Yoga. Just know Hatha Yoga is not the end of Yoga but the beginning. If you are very busy, a half hour a day is ideal along with an hour class once a week. What you put into your practice, will be returned to you. So make time each day. Consistency is important.

"Where shall I find a Hatha Yoga class?"

Call your YWCA, YMCA, Jewish Community Center or Adult Education program. (Classes are relatively inexpensive ranging from $1.00 to $3.00 per class.) Usually they have fine qualified teachers). A teacher should be the example of what she is teaching. You should feel uplifted, calmer, optimistic, and challenged after class. You will find there a lovely group of men, women and young people. Go and enjoy yourself. This is all part of the adventure!

"Do you teach your children Hatha Yoga?"

At this point, my children are young. We have fun together in a relaxed approach to Hatha Yoga. Rolling around in Bow is more "fun" for my eight-year-old than the formal class, although I have seen four-to-five-year-olds from a Montessori Yoga Class participate and benefit from a formal class.

Teaching the children to "relax" to sleep in "Sponge" is important. Sometimes after an exciting, long day of school, football, etc., both of my children have difficulty sleeping. So after prayer time, I take them through a simplified relaxation from their toes to their head. They love it.

The only prerequisite in showing your children this relaxation is that you should first know how to completely relax. Sponge is not an easy posture to do. By worldly standards, you look as if you are doing nothing. Observe how much more deeply the children will experience total relaxation after one month's practice. They, too, can learn from their own subtle, but direct experience, body control. Please do not confuse this with hypnosis. It is auto suggestion. The person who is "in relaxation" is in complete control over himself and nobody has control over him.

"What about Hatha Yoga and Mental Health?"

Very little is written about preventing mental illness and a great deal of attention is given after the fact. To me, Hatha Yoga is the finest form of preventive medicine for mental health. It is inexpensive too! How wonderful if this were taught in grammar school on up . . . .

If you suffer mentally, please do not feel alone. Each of us has our share of anxiety or depression. Yoga teaches you how to approach it and what to do with it.

Often psychiatry can be the most wonderful experience that could happen to a person.

Just know that a combination of Hatha Yoga and therapy might be of tremendous help. Your body will become stronger. Fatigue, due to emotional drain, will vanish. Your creative energy will focus on high, positive thinking, leaving the lower negative thoughts dormant. All of us must choose our Hatha Yoga teachers wisely! Someone who leads a vigorous, calisthenic type of class might suit you later, but not now. Look for a degree of warmth, cheerfulness and serenity in your instructor. There are many who really care.

Also, the whole subject of Hatha Yoga and Yogic philosophy might be an exciting subject to look forward to exploring further when you are through with therapy.

For Men Only

"Sometimes one seems to be talking only to women. Have you forgotten us men?"

No, my friends, I haven't forgotten you. I do know you are there. Some I picture as students, others the businessmen or others as grandfathers. You are a very important part of my Hatha Yoga class! Perhaps a little of what you hear is the result of my years of teaching "lady" classes (sprinkled occasionally with a few men).

It is very understandable why some men feel self-conscious in a live class with all those wonderful leotarded ladies. This feeling passes quickly as you close your eyes and start to work on yourself. A good teacher will help everyone lose self-consciousness quickly!

One of the most important and exciting benefits from Hatha Yoga for men, is that you, either as a man in business or a student, can put it into your daily life.

Take some of the postures and breathing into your office or classroom or on your business trip. Stop at some point during the morning coffee break. Get up! Close the door and do a modified stretch. Hold the stretch up to the ceiling and relax while standing. Stretch now from side to side. Hold the position. Release and stand straight. Feel how the energy flows where the tension had been building up. Breathe deeply and slowly. Suggest firmly to yourself that you are bringing new energy into the body as you inhale. As you exhale, out go all tension and tiredness. Teach yourself the art of taking minute vacations.

I used to think my husband's business trips were glamorous, then I accompanied him on a few. Strange hours, different beds, overcooked, heavy

food are what I found. I watched how hard he worked through the day and on into the dinner hour. It made me much more sympathetic to his problems and needs. I saw the need to break the business day with the "need some time for me" currents. One of my male students told me his remedy for travel fatigue. After the business day and before dinner, he said he placed a towel on the hotel rug and did a half hour of Hatha Yoga

Asanas with some breathing, with a five-minute relaxation at the end. Then a quick shower and off to the business dinner, feeling refreshed, energetic.

Take a little bit of time each day for yourself alone. Take time to energize your inner batteries. Anticipate your fatigue and tension needs before they happen. Use this Hatha Yoga in your everyday life!

Books About Yoga

I have listed a few books that continue to help me. Everyone is in a different phase of progress, so, if I have not suggested anything that appeals to you, go to your library or send away for a list and choose your own.

Book List

For the beginner in Hatha Yoga:

"Yoga, Youth & Reincarnation" by Jesse Stearns, Bantam Books $1.25

"Renew Your Life Through Yoga" by Indra Devi, Paperback Library (65-128)

"Be Young with Yoga" by Richard Hittelman, Paperback Library (54-394)

"Yoga for Beauty and Health" by Eugene Rowls and Eve Diskin, Paperback Library (55-740)

Books for Teachers

"Light on Yoga" (introduction only) by B. K. Iyengar, George Allen & Unwin, Ltd.

"The Complete Illustrated Book of Yoga" by Swami Vishnudevananda, Julian Press, Inc. Publishers, New York

Especially for men and professional people

"Executive Yoga" by Archie J. Bahm, Paperback Library $1.25 (66-30F)

Cookbooks

"Yogi Cookbook" by Yogi Vitaldas, Crown Publishers

"Gourmet Health Foods Cookbook" by Mike and Olga Teichner, Paperback Library, Easy-to-cookbook $1.75 (64-222)

"Let's Cook It Right" by Adelle Davis, Harcourt Brace and World

Those interested in all branches of Yoga philosophy

"The Sermon on the Mount According to Vedanta" by Swami Prabhauananda, Vedanta Press, 1946, Vedanta Place*, Hollywood, Calif. 90028

"The Bhagavadgita" translation by Radhakrisana, Vedanta Press, 1946, Hollywood, Calif. 90028

"Christian Yoga" by J. M., OSB Harper & Brothers, New York

"Introduction to Yoga and Its Principles and Practices" by Sachindra Kumiar Majumdar, University Books, New Hyde Park, New York

*Vedanta Press has a very complete book list and lovely sandalwood incense.

Breathing
(Pranayama)

Breathing is a science in itself. In this book, I have only scratched the surface of this valuable subject.

Here are a few random thoughts and hints. Breathe through your nose. Check during the day to see how much "mouth breathing" you are doing. The nose is nature's filter for pollution and smoking. It warms up cold air before it hits the lungs. Do not raise the shoulders when breathing. Expand entire rib cage.

Some say the breath is the bridge between the body and soul. Breath and body move together. Breath and mind should also move together. If your emotional state is agitated, your breath will be shallow and irregular. Calm the breath with rhythmical nose breathing. Your mind will also become quieter. Breath is energy. Breath is vitality. Breath is life.

Bhramari Breath

Exhale slowly through nose making humming sound, mind focused on sound.
Inhale through nose with high sound of bee.
Repeat three times.

Benefits:
Focuses attention and reminds us that body and breath move together. Strengthens concentration. Uses sound as a tool. Imparts a gentle feeling of peace and balance. Voice becomes sweet and melodious.
Excellent for senior adults and absolute beginners. If you cannot make first sound with ease, only do the hum.

Sniffing and Vitalic Breath

Breathe in through nose a series of sharp sniffs until lungs are completely full. Blow out sharply through mouth with loud HAAA. Cleans and strengthens lungs. Notice immediate warmth in face.

Simple Kapalabhathi

Mouth closed. Pretend you are going to sneeze. Inhale and sneeze. Keep head straight. Action in lower abdomen.
Do not try to breathe consciously. Balloon out abdomen, snap it back in sharply. Repeat (in-out) 10 times (one round). Repeat one more round (10 times). Work up to 50 comfortably.
You should feel no discomfort in upper lungs

such as a soreness or heat. STOP. We are not in a race!

Focus Attention on abdominal area. After breath is completed sit and observe the effects on body and mind.

Benefits:

Cleans respiratory system and nasal passages. Asthma is relieved. Tremendous for "pumping" oxygen into the system. Soothingly affects our skin and glands.

The Count

All through this book, I ask for different "counts" for breathing and the exercises. Try not to rush this count. Use OM-1, OM-2, OM-3 or one second one. Sometimes I have taken a watch with a second hand and checked it with myself, so as not to rush these counts and holds.

Alternate Breath
(Analoma-Viloma Pranayama)

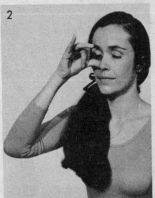

Sit straight, spine erect, head straight.

1. Using right hand, place second and third finger to center of palm.

2. Close right nostril with right thumb (exhale all air from left nostril).

Inhale slowly through left nostril, counting to four. Keep your mind focused on flow of air.

3. Retain breath to count of four. Pinch nostrils together gently with ring finger and thumb. Exhale slowly through right nostril to count of eight. Lift up thumb. Close the left nostril with ring finger and little finger. Completely remove all air from lungs on this long count.

4. Inhale through right nostril, count of four.

Retain breath to count of four. Gently pinch both nostrils together with thumb and little finger plus ring finger.

Exhale to count of eight, slowly through left nostril, lifting little and ring finger.

Repeat a complete round. In—hold—out—five times.

30

Benefits:

Natural tranquilizer. Calms nerves, relieves emotional tension and irritability. Quiets mind. Helpful before bedtime. Excellent before meditation.

Inhale left nostril	4 counts
Retain (both nostrils pinched lightly)	4 counts
Exhale right nostril	8 counts
Inhale right nostril	4 counts
Retain (both nostrils pinched lightly)	4 counts
Exhale left nostril	8 counts

Hints: Use complete breath 1—2—3 during inhalation and exhalation. As you become comfortable and practiced (one month) with this breath, you may attempt 4 in—16 hold—8 out. Your exhalation should always be longer than inhalation. Do not lengthen this count any more than 4—8—16, until you are under the personal guidance of a teacher.

Deep Abdominal Breath
(Complete Breath)

Breathe through nose. Mouth closed. Relax body. (First exhale all air)

Inhale
1. Balloon out abdomen slightly.
2. Expand middle rib cage.
3. Expand upper lungs. Hold. (Relax your face.)

Exhale
1. Release air slowly. Exhale air from upper lobes of lungs.
2. Middle rib cage.
3. Slightly contract abdominal muscles. Squeeze all stale air out. Repeat.

Repeat six times. As you become more aware of this breath and the lungs become stronger, work breath up to inhale count of 6. Do this complete breath during all postures when asked. Do during your working day!!

Benefits:
Increases oxygen supply into the blood, calming effect on nervous system. Slows down activity of the heart.

Observations:
When breathing is uneven, the mind is usually restless.

A Small Note to
Hatha Yoga Teachers

Little did I know a few years ago when I gave my first Hatha Yoga class where this form of service would lead. I know many of you feel the same way.

Reading has been of tremendous value to me. Eventually, we put down the reading and start the "doing". A book I highly recommend especially for its introduction is "Light on Yoga" by B. K. S. Iyengar. (George Allen and Unwin, Ltd.) The postures and breathing are a very different approach and technique. I would not advise use of the postures in class unless so trained. However, the introduction is clarity itself. It outlines to perfection the eight steps of Yoga. It explains with brilliance the ethical disciplines, the great commandments, transcending creed, country, age and time.

Here in Ohio, teachers get together to exchange viewpoints in periodical meetings and Yoga retreats. It has been a wonderful experience in sharing, in giving and receiving.

It took me a year of teaching to realize that I was learning more than the students. Once again I was reminded that we are all students walking this path together.

Please write me, I'd enjoy hearing from each of you. Bless you all.

Sponge – Relaxation Pose

(Savasana)

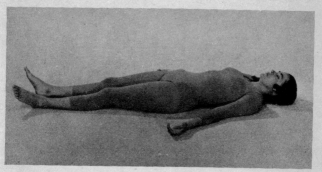

Lie on your back, feet slightly apart, hands at sides, palms turned upwards.

Eyes are closed.

Breathing is through nose, normal rhythm. Peaceful and relaxed.

Check your body for hidden tension in legs, face, hands, shoulders.

Observe what you have brought with you to class: tiredness, tension, inner restlessness.

Give firm positive suggestion to the removal of all negatives, replacing them with lightness, serenity, all that is uplifting and positive.

Relax each part of the body starting at toes and work up to forehead. Do not rush. Spend time on toes, legs, etc.

Pointers:

This is one of the more difficult postures to do well. To the world you look asleep, but inwardly you are alert and awake. Keep inner talking to a minimum with positive suggestion. Sponge is done between each asana.

Benefits:

Aids against insomnia and nervous tension.

Tension Relieving

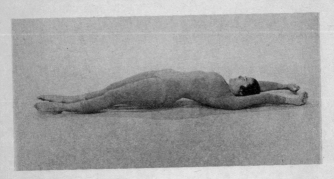

Lie flat on back.

Inhale to count of 5.

Raise arms over head till hands touch floor.

Make two separate fists. Raise buttocks off floor and tense and stretch every muscle of body. Tensing face is very important, shoulders, thighs, feet, buttocks.

Hold for count of 5.

Release breath, relax body, keep arms over head. Relax fingers.

Eyes are closed. Observe.

Let all tension and tiredness drain out of toes.

Repeat procedure, resting in Sponge in between.

Pointers:

Learn to increase the amount of time of the hold, according to your own capacity. Where we have tension (seen and unseen) in the body, we will have tiredness. When left unchecked, energy goes to feed tension.

Benefits:

As you become more aware of hidden tension and its removal, you will have more energy and vitality. Helps to prevent insomnia.

Warmups

These warmups, though tedious, are very important.

Immediately, they pave the road toward the Asanas.

They should be done three times each side.

Breathing is through nose. Inhaling as legs go up, exhale down.

Variations on the Alternate Leg Raise

Be sure to press back into floor as you raise legs. All movement proceeds from center of back without straining muscles.

Alternate Leg Raise to count of 5

1. Lie down. Inhaling to count of 5 with knee straight, slowly raise one leg 90°. Exhale. Lower leg to floor. Repeat 5 times each leg. Bhramari breath is helpful reminder to have movement and breath move together.

2. Both legs raise 90°. Lie down. Inhaling slowly to count of 5, raise both legs up to ceiling. Arms in T position, palms flat to floor. Hold comfortably. Exhale slowly to count of 5. Both legs down. Repeat 5 times.

3. Both legs raise 90° to "V". Lie down. Inhale slowly to count of 5. Raise both legs to ceiling. Exhale air. Inhale, legs apart. Exhale, legs together. Repeat "V" three times. Inhale, lower legs to floor gradually. Excellent for firming inside of thighs.

2

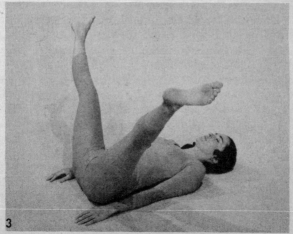

3

4. Knees side to side. Lie down. Arms in T position, palms down. Inhale. Bend both knees to chest. Exhale, bring both knees down to floor high under arm. Keep shoulders on floor. Look over opposite shoulder. Hold for 5 seconds. Breathe shallowly. Inhale. Repeat on opposite side. Check to see that both shoulders are on floor. Repeat 5 times rhythmically.

5. One knee to floor. Lie down. Feet together. Bring right foot sole on top of left thigh. Arms in T position. Palms down. Slowly lower right knee to left onto floor. Shoulders on floor. Look over opposite shoulder. Hold for 10 seconds. Relax. Bring right knee to start position. Change. Sole of left foot on top of right thigh. Slowly bring left knee to floor. Hold for 10 seconds. Relax. Let nature gradually stretch you out. Wonderful for waist and relief of tension in lower back.

6. Alternate side leg raise. Lie down. Arms extended. Palms down. Inhale to count of 5, raise right leg as high as possible. Exhale to count of 5, lower right foot to left hand. Do not rush! Hold for 5 seconds. Relax. Inhale, raise leg up to ceiling. Exhale. Lower leg to floor. Count of 5. Repeat with left leg. Repeat 3 times each leg. Work up to 5 times.

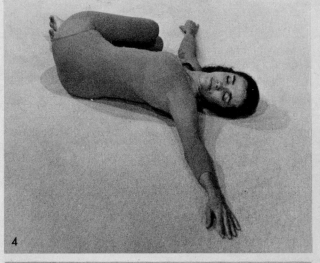

4

5

6

7. Repeat as above using both legs together. Do not worry if you do not connect toe with hand. Just try. It is the stretch and the strengthening action for the back that is important. A real abdomen firmer!

Hints:
Beginners move too fast—working the knees, using all muscles of the body (including face to raise the leg). Move slowly and continuously. Work up to 10 times each side.

Benefits:
Efficient way of pumping fresh blood through the body, essential pre-conditioner for Asanas (postures). Never strain. Bhramari breathing on all exhalation is very helpful.

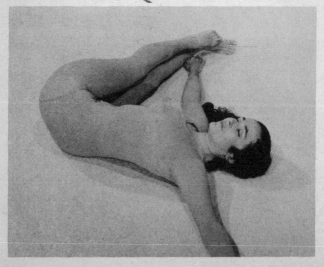

Toe to Forehead Stretch

Sit upright, legs extended.

Bend right leg at knee. Clasp right ankle. Right hand underneath right ankle. Left hand firmly around arch of right foot.

Draw your right foot up to touch your nose. Hold 5 seconds. Working to 30 seconds.

Lower leg slowly and repeat movement with opposite leg. Perform three times on each leg.

Pointers:

Many will not be able to bring toe to nose at first, indicating an unnatural tightness. Bring foot up as high as it will go, then hold.

Doing all Hatha Yoga exercises, normal flexibility will return.

Bend head forward if you cannot perform with straight back. Straighten back gradually.

Knee to Chest

Bend right knee to chest.
Arms over mid-lower leg.
Inhale, then exhale, bringing forehead to knee.
Press thigh against abdomen.
Hold, breathe shallowly, count to 5, release.
Return to Sponge. Relax. Observe inner tingling, on right side and left.
Repeat same on left knee bend.
Repeat procedures 2 times each side.

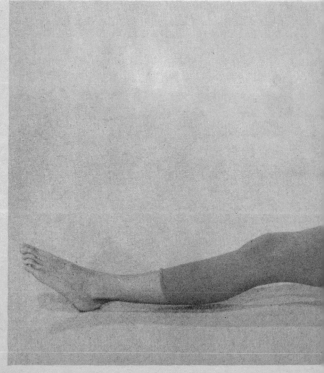

Pointers:

Press thigh to abdomen. There is slight pressure on inner vital organs. When you release, a fresh supply of blood goes to area stimulating inner organs.

Benefits:

Tones inner organs. Relieves gas. Increases spinal flexibility and stamina.

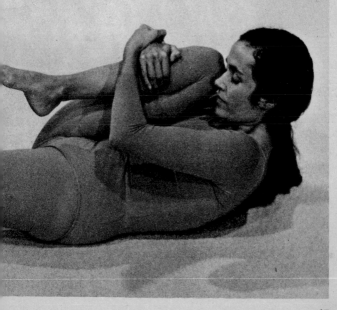

Rock 'n Roll 1.

Sit straight up. Bring knees to chest, arms around mid-lower legs.

Inhale and then exhale. Rock backwards. Inhale, rock forwards.

Rock on rounded spine, getting into small of back.

Do six times keeping an easy but vigorous movement.

Relax in Sponge. Observe different changes in spine and back muscles.

Pointers:
Have protection for your spine. Use rug or soft mat. Never on hard floor. Take care not to rock too high on upper neck vertebra.

Pay attention to breathing with the rocking motion. Inhale as you rock forward, exhale backwards.

Benefits:
Massages and tones muscles and nerves in the back and spine.

Keeps the spine flexible. Feels wonderful!

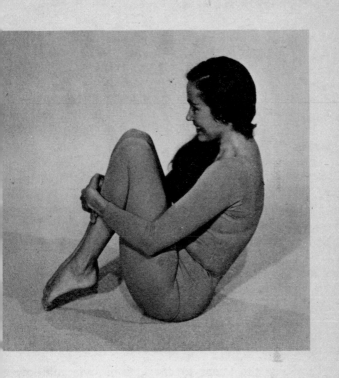

Rock 'n Roll 2.

(Intermediate) Cross ankles, hands over instep.
Holding ankles, inhale and exhale, rock back on
rounded spine.

Inhale, rock forward, bringing head close to
floor, still holding feet.

Do six times. With control and vigor, return to
Sponge. Observe warmth. Relax.

Benefits:
Added stretch to spine. Massages and tones
nerves and spinal cord.

If you are proficient in No. 1, you may roll higher
on upper shoulders.

Check padding on floor. You should feel no discomfort.

Rock 'n Roll 3.

Keep the knees to chest, arms over mid-lower
legs, roll from right elbow to left elbow.

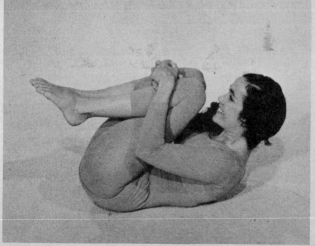

Eye Exercises

Beginners, do gradually, please!

1. Keeping face forward, move eyes to right, as far as possible. Then swing eyes to left. Alternate 3 times. (Working gradually to 5.)

Close for 10 seconds rest.

2. Repeat. Raise eyes, look up to ceiling. Down to floor. Three times, close and rest.

Roll eyes slowly. Make a complete circle. There should be no strain or pain. Make two complete circles in each direction.

End by palming eyes. Resting palms of hands on closed eyelids, fingers pointing upwards. Hold half minute.

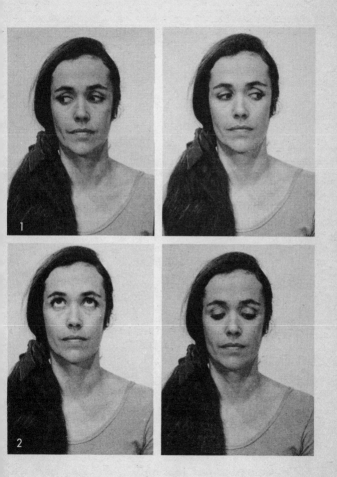

Foot Exercises

Kneel, buttocks on heels, top of feet flat on floor, toes pointing to rear. Let the weight of your body gently stretch ankles and feet.

Turn toes under, buttocks on heels. Let weight of your body stretch ankles and toes.

Sit on knees and heels. Place hands behind you. Support yourself well.

Gently roll back on your feet and toes. Do carefully. You control amount of weight on your feet.

Afterthoughts:

We remember our feet only when they hurt us. When our feet are sore, we are sore all over. Take your shoes off when possible. Do all Hatha Yoga exercises in bare feet. Shoes are necessary but constricting.

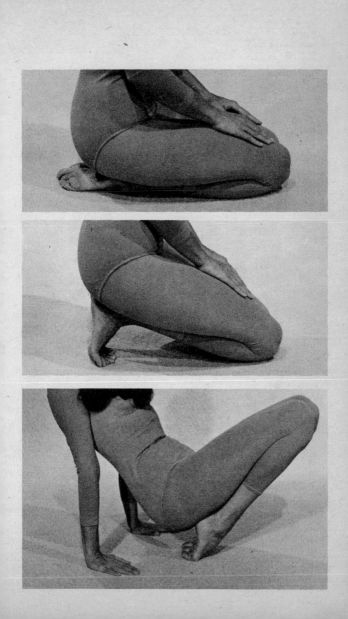

Cat Stretch

1. Kneel on hands and knees. Back straight, parallel to floor, arms and legs perpendicular, like a table. Palms flat.
2. Exhale, lower chest to floor. Rest chin on floor. Hold 5 seconds.
3. Inhale, in one flowing motion return to table position, then arch back like a cat. Pull stomach up toward spine. Hold. Release, relax spine and abdomen. Repeat twice.

Variation:
Kneel on hands and knees in "table" position. Back straight.
Inhale, raise right leg back and up. Head high. Exhale, bring knee to nose. Round the back. Repeat on other side.

Benefits:
Tremendous back strengthener. Obstetricians give this exercise after childbirth, it is effective in returning uterus to normal position and alleviating female complaints. Neck stretch firms jaw lines.
54

Neck Roll

1. and 2. Allow head to droop forward. Chin to chest. Hold 5 seconds. Inhale. Raise chin. Let your head hang back. Hold 5 seconds. Mouth closed. Exhale. Repeat twice.

3. and 4. Head straight. Exhale, lower head to right shoulder. Hold 5 seconds. Inhale and slowly raise head. Exhale, lower head to left shoulder. Hold 5 seconds. Inhale, head straight. (Be sure you are not bringing shoulder "up" to meet the head.) Repeat twice each side.

Beginners and people who have neck injuries, may place hands firmly on neck for extra support.

Note: Practice at odd moments, especially during prolonged desk sitting or at stop lights. If faithfully pursued, the gritty sound heard in neck will disappear. Stiffness and tension in neck is relieved when properly done.

Inhale, lifting chin high, mouth closed; slowly rotate head all the way around, allowing it to hang down in front, to the right, in back and to left. Do not turn face but allow head itself to relax and turn as the sunflower follows the sun. Repeat three or four times if necessary, rotating in reverse direction.

Rock a' Baby

To be done before attempting half or full lotus.
Sit upright, legs extended.
Grasp right foot, bring foot into inside of left elbow.
Wrap right arm around right knee. Clasp hands together.
Rock leg slowly from side to side.
Repeat with left leg.

Pointers:
Hold foot with both hands, if you cannot wrap arm around knee, make your own variation. Soon you will be able to do it!

Benefits:
Wonderful for loosening up hips, knees and ankles.

Easy Posture
(Sikhasana)

Sit upright. "Tailor fashion", knees bent, ankles crossed, soles upward. Spine is straight, hands resting easily on knees in Jnana Mudra hand position, (palms turned up, thumb and index finger touching, symbolizing the universe).

Pointers:

Be comfortable! It is a posture for periods of prayer and meditation. I find sitting on a pillow (buttocks on pillow, ankles on a rug) helpful for those moments. If knees do not touch ground, do not worry.

Benefits:

Wonderful discipline in learning the art of sitting quietly. Whether it's sitting in your office or listening to a friend's conversation, in any situation, use your Hatha Yoga! You bring tranquillity and control into the situation.

Half Lotus
(Ardha-Padmasana)

Sit upright, legs extended, bend right knee, bring right foot as high as possible on top of left thigh. Sole upward.

Keep right knee close to floor.

Bend left knee, slide left foot under right thigh, sole upward.

Both knees are as close to the floor as possible.

Spine straight, with hands resting on knees, fingers assume Jnana Mudra hand position. Repeat on opposite side.

Benefits:

Returns youthful flexibility to ankles, knees and thighs.

Caution: If there is pain anywhere, STOP. Get to know difference between pain and stretch! Not for sufferers of acute varicose veins.

Full Lotus
(Padmasana)

Sit upright, legs extended.

Clasp right foot, placing it high on top of left thigh.

Bend left knee, edge left foot close to FRONT of right calf.

Carefully clasp left ankle and gently bring foot over right calf and up high on thigh.

Place hands gently on knees, fingers assuming Jnana Mudra.

Hold position for a few seconds.

Release carefully, unfolding feet from thighs.

Repeat full lotus on opposite side beginning with left foot on top of right thigh.

Pointers:

Do all knee warmups first. Treat your knees gently. Never yank your knees into this position. Gradually both knees will loosen up to touch floor.

Benefits:

Tones nerves and circulates blood in the lower lumbar region and abdomen. Relieves stiffness and tension in back, knees and ankles. Challenging to do.

Side Comment:

Some of the best teachers and students of Yoga cannot do this position. It has never held back their spiritual progress, however! Do not sit for long periods of time in this position. It is for the Indians who have been sitting this way since childhood.

Yoga Mudra

Sit in lotus or easy posture.

Interlock fingers behind back. Straighten elbows.

1. Raise your chin up to ceiling, pressure on upper vertebra.

Inhale through nose.

Continue pressure on back of neck. Slowly lower head to floor. Exhale slowly. Tuck chin under forehead on floor. Slowly return to Position 1.

Inhale and release both slowly.

2. Raise arms behind you, hands still clasped as high as possible, elbows straight. Hold 10 sec-onds. Breathe normally.

Inhale. Raise head (pressure on upper vertebra). Return to Position 1. slowly. Release. Close eyes. Observe feelings in shoulders, arms and face.

Repeat procedure once more. Relax in Sponge.

Pointers:

Do slowly. Raise straightened arms only as far as you can. Practice will loosen this up. Release position slowly!

Benefits:

Dramatically releases tension of the day which settles in shoulders. Yoga Mudra helps constipation problems.

64

1

2

Arrow Balance 1.

Sitting position.
Hug both knees to chest, arms wrapped around front of lower leg.
Straighten spine.
Raise toes up and balance. Hold, breathe shallowly to count of 10.

Benefits:
Strengthens abdomen and thigh muscles. Balancing calms a restless mind.

Arrow Balance 2.

Same as 1.
Wrap arms around front of knees. Raise toes and balance.
Loosen right arm, hold straight out to side. Loosen left arm, hold straight out to side.
Hold for count of 6. Spine straight. Knees close to chest. Breathe shallowly. Return to easy posture.

Pointers:
Keep mind focused on the body's balancing point.

Caution:
If you lose balance, round the spine, and roll back on your soft mat.

Arrow Balance 3.

Sitting straight in easy posture.
Firmly clasp right and left ankle with hands.
Hold on to ankles and straighten legs, knee caps tight, legs pointing to ceiling.
Balance. Keep back straight. Hold.
Return to sitting position slowly and peacefully.

Simple Twist 1.
(Ardha Matsyendrasana)

Sit on knees. Place left hand around outside of right thigh. Fingers locked (between calf and thigh of right leg).

Inhale through nose, making a long sweep behind you with your right arm.

Bring right hand around your back to touch waist or left thigh.

Exhale. Inhale. Focus eyes over right shoulder, use locked hand as leverage, giving your spine a safe low lateral twist.

Breathe normally. Hold for 5 seconds working to 15 seconds.

Repeat twist, reversing sides.

Benefits:

Trims the waist. Tonic for nervous system and relieves deep tension in back and spine.

Pointer:

This may be performed sitting in chair with legs crossed if you cannot sit on floor.

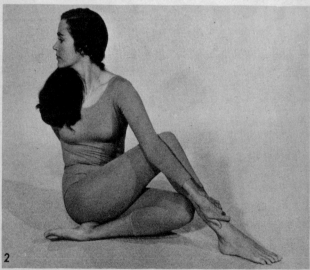

Spinal Twist 2.

Place sole of left foot against inside of right thigh. Heel as close to groin as possible.

1. Bend right knee. Bring right foot over left knee. Right foot flat on floor. Hook left shoulder and arm over right knee. Grasp right ankle.

2. With right arm making a large arc, grasp waist.

Focus eyes on wall over right shoulder.

Hold position for 5 seconds, breathing normally. Do only once.

Release and repeat, alternating sides, reversing hands, legs twisting to left.

Pointers:
If you cannot reach your ankle or calf, simply hold knee with left hand. Add a few seconds each week until you are holding up to 30 seconds.

Afterthoughts:
Twist is slightly complicated but fun and feels delightful.

Benefits:
Removes deep tension in back and spine. Hip joints are limbered. Reduces fat at waistline.

Camel 1.
(Ustrasana) Pelvic Stretch

Sit on heels. Place palms on floor behind feet, fingertips facing wall behind you.

Drop head back loosely. Place weight on hands.

Inhaling deeply, raise buttocks off heels, arching back, pelvis thrust forward.

Hold this position, breathing normally for 10 seconds.

Return to sitting position.

Rest with eyes closed. Inhale deeply through nose. Exhale deeply through nose. Repeat once more.

Pointers:
Experience this posture and its relaxing effect. Do movement slowly and gracefully. In holding, be like a motionless statue.

Benefits:
Camels provide stretching and limbering of toes, ankles and feet. Excellent stretch of spine and upper thigh muscles.

Develops bust line.

Camel 2.

(Ustrasana) Pelvic Stretch

Kneel on floor, knees slightly apart, feet apart.

Lean back carefully. Grasp one heel, then the other.

Arch back, head back, neck loose. Mouth closed. Eyes closed.

Hold for 10 seconds. Breathe normally.

With eyes closed, observe different stretches, temperature changes.

Repeat process once more. Go right into Folded Leaf (See page 102).

Lie down, relax.

Pointers:
Reach back, get a firm hold on one heel, then try for the other.

Benefits:
Stretches lower back. Benefits female organs. Upper thigh muscles receive added stretch.

Caution:
Not for students suffering from hernia or for those who have had abdominal surgery.

Warrior Posture
with Over Shoulder Hand Clasp

Sit upright, legs straight in front.
Bend left knee over right thigh, right hand clasping left instep.
Bend right knee, left hand clasping left instep.
Raise left arm over head as if to scratch spine. Lower right arm, bending at elbow, and raise forearm up behind back until two hands touch.
Clasp hands firmly. Head erect. Hold pose for 30 seconds breathing normally.
Unclasp hands. Straighten legs and repeat pose on the other side.
Relax in Sponge.

Benefits:

Helps with leg cramps and keeps muscles elastic. Chest is well expanded.

Pointers:

If you cannot clasp both hands together, throw a handkerchief over your shoulders holding fast to end. Bring opposite hand up to catch a corner.

The more upright you keep upraised arm, the better the results.

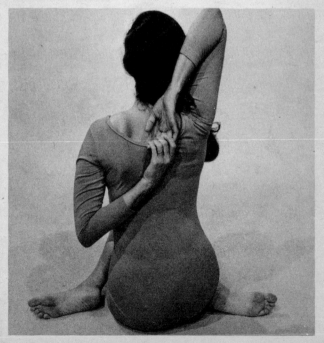

Atlas Posture

Sit upright on heels, knees together, hands at sides.

Inhale through nose, raise arms over head, clasp fingers together, slide on to right buttock.

Exhale through nose, arch to left.

Hold for count of six, relax. Breathe shallowly.

Inhale through nose. Come up to sitting position on heels.

Repeat stretch to left.

Reverse position. Slide on left buttock and stretch to right.

Repeat twice.

Pointers:

Do carefully and slowly.

Keep concentration on the parts of the body which are being stretched.

Head stays between upper arms.

Benefits:

Wonderful for reducing waistline and stretching ribs. Increases spinal flexibility.

Lion Posture
(Simhasana)

Sit on heels. Knees slightly apart. Palms on knees.

Inhale deeply through nose, hold breath, rise off heels as if about to pounce.

All together 1—5

1. Exhale air through open mouth.
2. Stick tongue out.
3. Stretch fingers and spread far apart.
4. Eyes wide open. Eyebrows up.
5. Make a "Haa" sound.

Hold for a few seconds.

Release. Close eyes. Observe the warmth in face and neck area. Repeat twice.

Pointers and benefits:

I find this beneficial when I'm about to get a cold. Lion posture and salt water gargle repeated during day! You can do this sitting in your office (door closed), or standing in front of mirror in morning. Excellent before giving speeches. Lion brings blood to root of tongue. Some say it brings extra energy to brain.

Half Shoulder Stand
(Salamba Sarvangasana)

Lie down on your back, hands at sides, palms down, feet together.

Inhale slowly through nose, raise legs straight up to ceiling.

Exhale.

Inhale, raise your hips off the floor, using hands to push off.

Support yourself with hands cupped around hips, elbows on floor close together.

The face should feel heavy with fresh supply of blood.

Hold position for one minute. Breath is shallow and comfortable.

Slowly bend both knees to face, palms flat on floor, lower hips to floor. Keep head on floor. Do not collapse. Slowly lower legs to floor.

Relax in Sponge. Observe different changes in circulation.

Breathe normally.

Pointers:

One of the best to do each day. Especially when you are tired. Never collapse. Do slowly and gracefully. Gradually build up to hold of 5 minutes or longer. There should be no pain, only feeling of stretch.

Benefits:

Wonderful relief of fatigue. Helpful relief from varicose veins. Helps smooth out wrinkles. As you learn to hold ½ shoulder stand for over one minute, immediately go into beginner Fish pose. Relax in Sponge.

Full Shoulder Stand—Candle

(Niralamba Sarvangasana)

Lie flat on your back, feet together, palms flat on floor.

Inhale through nose, raise legs straight up to ceiling.

1. Exhale, press palms to floor, lift hips off floor, support your back firmly with hands. Keep elbows close together.

Move hands down toward shoulders. Chin is locked firmly in the throat. Pelvis is pushed forward.

Eyes closed. Observe the wonderful changes going on as you hold for one minute.

2. and 3. Slowly and with control, place hands firmly on mat for support, lower trunk of body to floor. Once hips touch ground, lower straightened legs to floor.

Relax in Sponge. Observe carefully, different coolness, temperature change, release of tension.

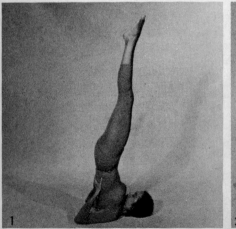

Pointers:

Never collapse returning to Sponge. If you cannot come down without collapsing, bend knees to forehead, support yourself with palms flat on mat. Roll down slowly, legs together, keep head on floor.

Once hips touch floor, straighten legs, return slowly to Sponge.

With continued practice and retaining position, you will become stronger. Work up to a hold of 5 to 10 minutes.

Benefits:

Tones entire system. Increases stamina. After a long day on your feet, raise yourself to shoulder stand. Gravity is reversed, allowing relief for tired feet and legs. Thyroid and parathyroid areas get a slight squeeze, therefore it is important to do Fish immediately before returning to Sponge.

Beginner Fish 1.

(Matsyansana)

Lie on your back, legs together. Slide arms under your back.

Palms down, hands touching.

Arch back, raise chest off floor placing *all weight* on elbows.

Head bent back, only lightly touch ground.

Hold position for one minute. Breathe deeply and fully through nose.

Release posture. Relax in Sponge.

Caution:

Check to see weight is on elbows, not on back of head.

Muscles in neck are usually weak in beginning and should not take too much pressure at first. If there is a slight feeling of nausea, come out of position. This happens occasionally.

Benefits:

Fish has opposite effect from shoulder stand, opening up the thyroid area. Helpful for asthma sufferers.

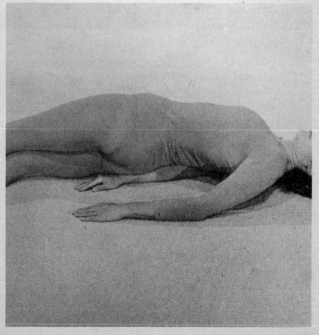

Intermediate Fish 2.
(Matsyansana)

Fish always follows shoulder stand.

Sit on heels, knees wide apart, drop to one elbow then to other elbow.

Arch back, lower top of head gently to ground.

Weight evenly on both elbows. Eyes closed. Mouth closed. Take three complete breaths. Hold for ½ minute. Work up to 2 minutes.

Release posture. Raise up on elbows. Straighten legs.

Relax in Sponge.

Pointers:

Approach Fish 2 slowly and carefully. Never force yourself into any asana. Knees should stay on floor. As you progress, bring knees closer and closer together. Check to see weight is on elbows.

Caution:

This is not an asana for beginners. If a feeling of nausea occurs, come out of posture. Return to Sponge. Take five complete breaths. The body rebels like a spoiled child. As you progress, this feeling of nausea goes away spontaneously. Rejoice.

Plough
(Halasana)

Lie in Sponge position. Feet together, arms at sides, palms down.

Inhale deeply, exhaling raise legs upward and over head until toes touch floor.

Feet together. Arms over head. Breathe shallowly. Hold position for 30 seconds.

Bend both knees to forehead. Return arms to floor. Lower your hips to floor, vertebra by vertebra.

Keep head on floor. Once hips touch floor, straighten legs. Lower legs together. Relax back in Sponge. Close eyes. Observe different feelings and changes inside body.

Pointers:

Bring your toes over your head only as far as you can go, keeping your balance. You will stretch out stiff muscles in time. No forcing, please! Do Plough only after six weeks of Hatha Yoga practice.

Benefits:

A tremendous energizer when fatigued. Lower backache relieved. Reduces abdominal weight. Spine receives extra supply of blood due to forward bend.

Afterthoughts:

When in Plough, difficulty in breathing sometimes occurs. As abdominal wall becomes stronger, inner abdominal organs are held up naturally, breathing difficulties will disappear.

Forward Bend 1.
(Paschimottanasana)

Sit upright with legs extended. Inhale, raise arms over head, stretch. Exhale.

Bend forward, forehead to your knees to your maximum stretch (no pain).

Relax your neck, shoulders. Place hands on calves if you cannot touch ankles.

Breathe evenly, shallowly, effortlessly.

Eyes closed.

Observe what muscles are talking back to you. Give firm and positive suggestion for them to relax.

Hold for ½ minute. Work up to 3—5 minutes.

Release. Lie down, relax.

Pointers:

Place hands on calves if you cannot touch ankles. Knees are straight, feet together. If your knees look a great distance away, have hope! Practice each day will return spinal and muscle flexibility. In two weeks it will be much easier.

Benefits:

Relieves tiredness in legs and lower back. Especially after a long day of sitting at a desk. Helps to firm flabby thighs.

Forward Bend—Intermediate 2.

(Paschimottanasana)

Same as 1. except:

Place two fingers between big toe and second toe. Slowly lower elbows to ground. Forehead to knees.

This should not be attempted until 1. is mastered easily. Do slowly.

Let nature gradually stretch muscles and ligaments.

No bouncing. Soon your forehead will be touching knees.

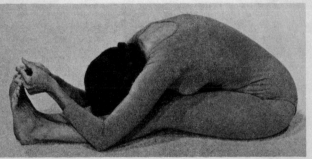

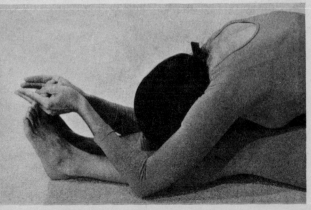

Backward Bend or Inclined Plane

(Puruottanasana)

Sitting upright, legs together, feet together. Close your eyes.

Place palms behind you flat on floor, fingers falling away from body.

Inhale through nose, raise hips up, head back. Relax neck. Keep heels together, palms flat.

Hold posture for count of 5. Hold breath.

Exhale through nose. Return to upright sitting position.

Repeat procedure one more time.

Resume Sponge posture. Observe inner changes.

Pointers:

After forward bend, always do inclined plane. For every forward posture, there is the opposite

movement. Remember Hatha Yoga is scientifically put together.

Benefits:
All of you who enjoy golf, tennis, or play a musical instrument, will find this beneficial in strengthening arms and wrists and shoulders.

Intermediate Only:
Raise body up to inclined plane, head back, palms flat on floor, fingertips toward back wall. Raise right leg, inhale, exhale down.
Inhale, left leg up. Exhale down.
Lie down, Relax.
Please do not practice until you have mastered 1. comfortably.

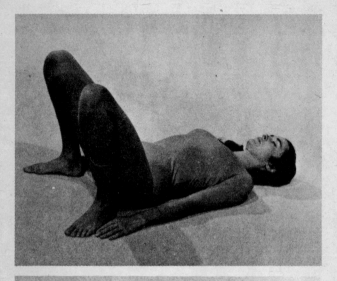

Bridge 1.

Lie on back. Bend both knees, heels touching buttock muscles.

Feet flat on floor.

Palms flat on floor. Press down with palms.

Inhale through nose; raise hips off ground, as pictured in Bridge 2. Hold six seconds. Exhale through nose; lower hips to ground. Repeat 3 times.

Bridge 2.

Lie on back. Bend both knees.

Reach back and grasp both ankles. Feet flat on floor.

Holding on to ankles, feet flat on floor, inhale through nose, raise hips.

Hold for 6 seconds. Exhale through nose; hips to floor. Repeat 3 times.

Benefits:

This should feel good! And help strengthen weak backs. (If there is a question about your back, check with your doctor.) Increases flexibility in lower back. Firms buttock area.

Bridge 3.

Lie on back. Bend both knees, bring feet as close as possible to buttocks, feet flat on floor. Inhale through nose; raise hips off floor.

Slip hands under small of back. Thumbs touching. Palms cupping hip bones. Slowly walk feet out till knees are straight. Shoulders are on mat. Elbows close.

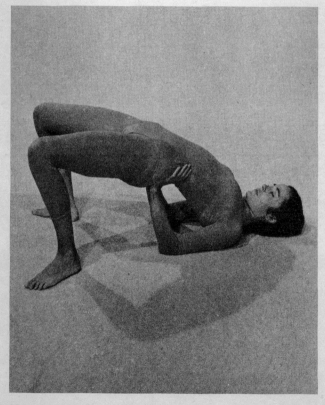

Pointers:

Not to be practiced before 1. and 2. are comfortable. Do slowly, walk as far as you can to straighten knees, then STOP, HOLD, relax. Never force anything.

Benefits:

Increased flexibility in lower back and spine. A challenge. It is worth mastering.

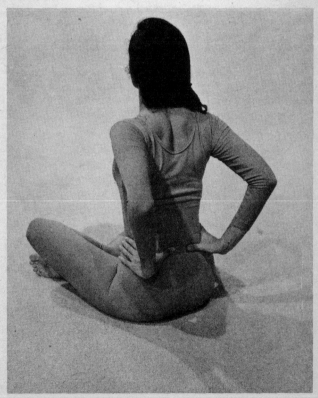

Half Locust
(Salabhasana)

Lie face down on mat. Hands along side, palms down. Feet together, chin on floor. Inhale. Raise left leg up. Knees straight. Hold for 5 seconds. Exhale, lower leg slowly to floor.

Inhale. Raise right leg up. Knees straight. Hold for 5 seconds.

Exhale. Lower leg slowly to floor.

Repeat process twice.

This is very important preparation for Full Locust.

Benefits:

Strengthens and firms muscles of lower back, upper thigh and abdomen. Rich supply of blood flushes the face and brain. Pelvic organs are invigorated.

Cobra, Locust and Bow follow one another.

Full Locust

Lie down on mat, fists clenched, bring straight arms under groin. Body straight, chin on floor. Check to see that inside of elbows are on floor.

Inhale deeply, thrust both legs up to ceiling. Hold for 5 seconds.

Release, exhale. Repeat once more.

Bring arms out from under you.

Relax. Deeply observe inner changes.

Eyes closed.

Pose of A Child
or Closed Leaf

Sit on heels, toes flat, forehead to floor, arms relaxed on either side of legs, palms up. Keep buttocks on heels. Completely relax in position.

Hold for one minute. Relax.

Benefits:

Excellent to do after vigorous lower back

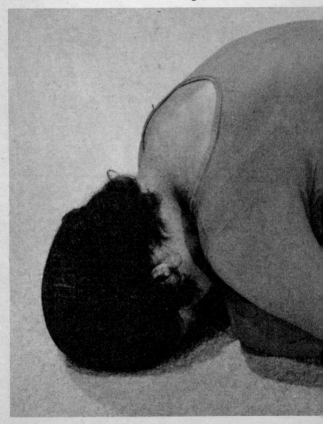

stretches; i.e., Cobra, Pelvic Stretch. Pose gives total relaxation in sitting position.

Breathe gently, eyes closed. Sit up.

Variations:

Bend forward with knees wide apart simulating an open leaf. Sit on heels.

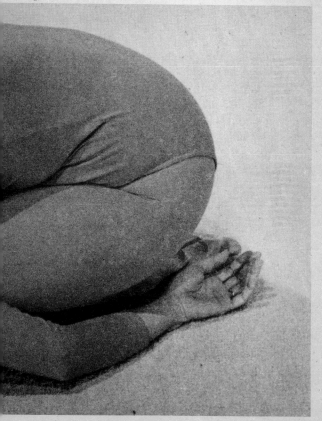

Cobra Posture
(Bhujangasana)

Lie face down on mat, feet together, toes pointed but relaxed.

Place hands directly under shoulders (fingers pointing forward).

Forehead to floor.

Slowly raise and let face skim floor:
1. forehead
2. nose
3. chin (pressure on upper neck vertebra)
4. shoulders
5. —10. Slowly raise upper and middle back, vertebra by vertebra.

Keep lower half of body, from hip down, on floor. Elbows slightly bent. Exhale down slowly.

Keep pressure on upper neck vertebra until head is lowered to floor.

Pointers:
Focus your attention on the spine as it rises vertebra by vertebra. Feel its snakelike motion as the spine rolls back. Be sure your count is slow. OM 1—OM 2—OM 3.

Benefits:
A complete stretch for spine, neck and shoulders. Develops chest and bust. Firms buttocks and arms. Activates thyroid areas.

Caution:
If hyperthyroid conditions exist, do not place pressure on upper neck. Keep head straight.

Advanced Cobra:
Up to Cobra to count of 30 and down to 30.

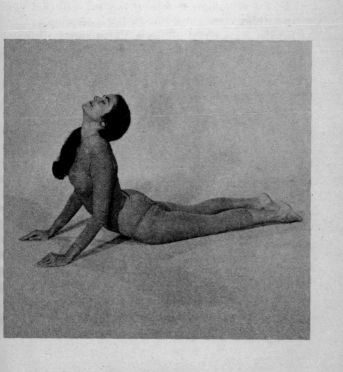

Bow
(Dhunurasana)

Lie on stomach, reach back and firmly clasp both ankles.

Inhale, raise chest off floor. Raise knees off floor.

Hold for 5 seconds. Release, but hold on to ankles.

Exhale. Repeat twice.

Pointers:
Knees are 2 feet apart. As you progress, bring them closer together. If you cannot clasp your ankles the first time . . . courage!

Get your wife or husband to help you. In a few weeks' time, with practice and other exercises, you will loosen up stubborn areas.

Benefits:
Bow is the combined effect of Cobra and Locust. Usually tried after six weeks of practice. Bow has subtle effects on glands, digestion and circulation. Stamina and inner resiliency are the friends of this posture. Worth working at. Do not collapse at end.

The Sun Salute
(Suryanamaskar)

 Palms together. Inhale and exhale.

Inhale. Stretch back. Arms in a V and head back. Arch back easily. Tighten buttock muscles so lower back will not take too much weight and cause irritation.

Keeping head between upper arms, slowly bend forward. Knees straight bending from waist. Relax head, neck, shoulders and arms. Exhale.

 Bend both knees. Place palms flat on either side of the feet. Right leg

back. Right knee on floor. Stretch chin up to the ceiling. Inhale.

 Both legs back. Body straight. Head looking at the wall in front of you. Retain breath.

 Toes, knees, chest, forehead on the floor (not abdomen!) Exhale!

Cobra posture. Inhale. Arch back the spine. Chin up to the ceiling. Hips on the floor. Elbows slightly bent. Toes on the floor.

 Jack-knife hips up to the ceiling. Heels to the floor. Chin locked in chest. Exhale!

Left leg up between the two hands. Right knee on the floor. Palms flat. Chin stretched to the ceiling. Inhale!

Both feet together, knees straight, bend forward from the hips. Relax neck, head, arms. Exhale!

Slowly raise arms to either side of the ears. Stretch hands towards the wall in front of you. Inhale slowly, stretch up to the ceiling, arching back slightly. Arms in a "V." Head back.

Exhale. Bring palms together. Eyes closed. Observe the different body changes.

Observe carefully the increase of heat, your breath, your heart beat.

Each of the twelve postures should be held three seconds. Once you become familiar with the sun salute, each asana (posture) will flow one into the other.

At first simply do two sun salutes using different legs. There should be no feeling of breathlessness. Above all, go slowly according to your own capacity. If there is a history of high blood pressure or heart trouble, please check with your doctor.

Head Stand

(Kapalasana)

Kneel on floor.

1. Place elbows on floor. Place head, middle of crown, on floor supporting head with cupped hands.

Straighten knees. Walk yourself in until weight is on elbows and hands. (Very little on head.) Just doing this has excellent benefits on the headstand. Remember to measure distance between elbows by a clenched fist and forearm. Interlace fingers. Place hands on floor, thumbs up.

Measure distance between elbows

Interlace

2

2. Contract muscles of abdomen, lift knee to chest. Hold, balance for a moment. Go no further! If you fall at this point, round your back and roll; no twisting.

Continue, only if you are not shaking or quivering.

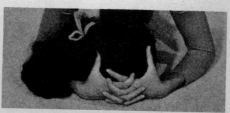

fingers   Hands on floor, thumbs up

3. Raise knees up until knees and lower legs are parallel to floor. Hold. Go no further if you feel dizziness. It is better and easier to come down quickly from this.

4. Knees completely straight and balance. Check to see weight is evenly on elbows, hands and head. Body should be straight, no sway. Breathing through nose is easy and even. Bend knees to chest slowly. Return feet to floor. Keep body in Pose of a Child for half minute.

3

Pointers:

Headstand is done in gradual, controlled stages. Do not use a wall. Soon your muscles will be your wall.

Practice on soft rug, so that if you lose balance, you roll from position II and do not twist.

Benefits:

Challenges your flexibility, balance and strength.

4

Abdominal Contraction or Stomach Lift
(Uddiyana Bandha)

Stand erect. Inhale deeply. Bend slightly forward, hands on thighs, and exhale forcefully (hum out last vestiges of air).

No air left in the lungs.

Pull the abdomen up and back to spine, pressing against rib cage.

Hold until air is needed. Release, stand straight. Relax.

Repeat twice.

Pointers:

There are two separate motions up and back.

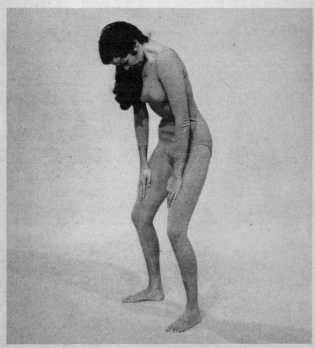

Practice on empty stomach. It is really worth the effort trying. Muscle tone and waistline will quickly improve.

Benefits:

For people with digestive problems. In your zeal to learn this at first, only do two or three times for first week.

Very powerful. Good for men whose abdomens hang over the belt a bit.

Excellent after childbirth when doctor gives you the go ahead.

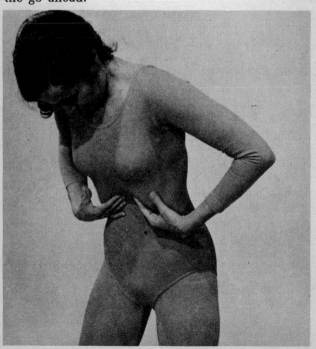

Eagle
(Gurudasana)

Stand straight. Bend right knee.

Wrap left leg over right thigh trying to hook left leg above inner side of right ankle.

Balance on right leg only.

Bend left elbow and raise arm to level of chest. Rest right elbow on left upper arm near elbow joint. Join palms together, arms entwined.

Repeat entire pose, reversing sides.

Pointers:

Learn to balance on entwined leg first before adding arm movement. Use chair or wall for balance if needed.

Benefits:

This asana develops ankles and removes shoulder stiffness. It is recommended for preventing calf cramps.

Triangle
(Trikonasana)

Stand upright, feet wide apart. Raise left arm up to ceiling (upper arm close to ear). Right hand resting on side of right thigh.

Bend to right, inching right hand slowly down side of leg to right ankle. Hold for 30 seconds at maximum point of stretch.

Breathe normally. Inhale deeply, return. Repeat procedure reversing sides.

Pointers and benefits:

Tones up thigh, calf and hamstring muscles. This pose increases blood supply around lower spine. Relieves pain in back and invigorates abdominal organs.

116

Tree Posture 1.
(Vrikshasana)

Stand on both feet, feet slightly apart, knees straight.

Lift right foot and place it high inside of left thigh.

Slowly raise arms over head. Palms together, elbows back.

Hold posture for 30 seconds. Take two complete breaths.

Lower arms. Lower foot to floor. Repeat entire posture reversing sides.

Pointers:

If you lose balance, use a wall or chair. Find a spot on wall, eye level, keep eyes focused there.

Benefits:

I love balancing. It gives us grace, inner and outer balance and control. A gentle strengthener of legs, ankles and feet.

Tree Posture 2.

Stand straight. Spine erect. Feet slightly apart.

Lift right foot and place high on left thigh. Sole is outward.

Raise arms over head. Place palms together. Stretch elbows back.

Hold position for one minute. Breathe deeply. Lower arms to sides.

Lower foot to floor. Repeat entire posture reversing sides.

Pointers:

Find a spot on wall. Eye level. Keep gaze there as you maneuver your body into Tree. Smile and try again if you jump around the first time.

Variation:

Place palms together. Straighten elbows. Stretch arms up to ceiling.

Woodchopper

Stand straight—legs apart, knees locked.

Clasp hands in front of you, interlacing fingers. Inhale deeply, through nose. Raise arms up to ceiling, being sure the movement of arms and breath are together. Stretch arms up as high as possible. Look up to ceiling. Hold for 5 seconds.

Exhale, vigorously through mouth, swing arms down, (elbows straight) through knees. Hold for 5 seconds. Relax head.

Inhale slowly up to standing position. Arms straight, hands clasped. Exhale.

Release hands. Relax in standing position. Repeat procedure three times.

Keep elbows and spine straight. Use your imagination. Feel the axe as it swings down in one powerful motion to split the wood. Movement should all be above the waist.

Benefits:

A nifty energizer! Keeps the spine flexible and reduces abdominal fat. The vigorous breath is excellent for a lung cleansing action.

Chest Expander 1.

Stand erect. Hands at sides. Feet 3 inches apart. Bring arms behind you.

Clasp hands. Straighten both arms out behind you as far as you can.

Tighten buttocks and knees. Inhale, expand your chest to its full capacity, raising chin to ceiling, squeezing upper neck gently. Hold comfortably. Relax. Close eyes. Release hands. Observe!

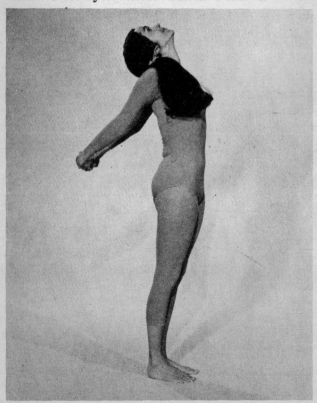

Chest Expander 2.

Repeat above process. Straighten both arms. Inhale deeply. Chin up to ceiling. Keep arms straight and up. Hold for 5 seconds. Release. Relax. Close eyes. Repeat twice!

Repeat 1. and 2.

Arms behind you. Clasp hands together. Inhale. Keep elbows straight. Hands firmly clasped behind you. Drop head back and arch back comfortably. Exhale, straighten up slowly. Without stopping, bend forward until head is as close to knees as possible. Arms forward as far as possible. Hold 10 seconds.

Slowly come up, not releasing arms until body is completely straight. Close eyes. Relax in standing position.

Benefits:

Releases tension in neck and shoulders. Good for trimming abdomen. Develops chest and muscles relating to bust.

Hints:

Do slowly. Have all movements flow into one another.

Keeping arms up as high as possible will increase benefits. When you wish to relieve pressure upon you, stop and do 1, 2, or 3. It can be better than that second cup of coffee.

Head to Knee
(Parsuottanasana)

Stand with legs wide apart. Place hands in Namaste position behind back, palms together between shoulder blades, fingers pointing upward. Place right foot at 90° angle.

Turn left foot slightly to right. Inhale, arch back, head back.

Exhale through nose. Bring forehead to right knee. Relax in position for 20 seconds. Breathe normally. Inhale, return.

Repeat entire pose in opposite direction. Lie down in Sponge. Relax.

Pointers:

If you cannot fold hands together behind back, just grip the wrist and follow above technique, slowly and in control. No bouncing. As you progress, you will come closer to the goal of forehead to knee.

Benefits:

People who cannot do headstand will find they can benefit from this pose. Increases blood circulation to head and trunk. Great for your complexion!

Namaste position.

Cow 1.

Stand erect. Feet 3 inches apart. Arms at side. Slowly drop chin to chest. Mentally picture each vertebra in upper neck "curling" forward. Take 20 seconds from upright to forward position.

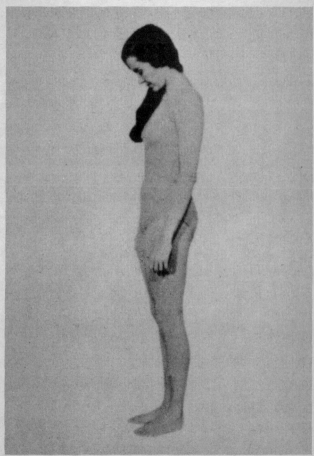

Cow 2.

Relax arms. Relax shoulders. Keep attention focused on vertebra between shoulders. Continue "curling" spine for 20 seconds. Face and arms close to body. Lock chin gently in notch top of breastbone. Relax. Let arms hang, no bouncing! Trunk hangs limply, pulling naturally against supporting muscles and tendons.

When body cannot be stretched further forward comfortably, clasp ankle or calf. Bend elbows. Slowly pull yourself to farthest comfortable limit. Aim forehead toward your knees. Hold for 10 seconds. Release legs and curl slowly (20 seconds) to upright in exactly the reverse manner you went down. Unlock chin last! Repeat exercise.

Benefits:

Increases circulation of blood in head and face. Easy to do. Affects spinal elasticity. Tendons in back of legs become more flexible.

Reminder:

A good one to do with street clothes on to relieve tension during your day.

Rishi Posture
Arm and Leg Stretch

Stand erect, etc. Slowly raise right arm. Palm holding up ceiling.

Pull left foot up behind you with left hand. Stretch arm back without losing balance. Slowly drop head back. Hold for 10 seconds. Release.

Slowly bring right arm forward; at same time release pull on left foot and thigh.

Stand normally. Repeat exercise on alternate side.

Raise left arm. Hold ceiling up with palm of hand. Bend right leg and clasp foot with right hand, etc.

Benefits:

Strengthens and stretches legs and arms. Challenges your inner and outer balance. Use a wall or chair at first, if you find yourself a bit wobbly.

Namaste
Indian Gesture of Respect

Palms of the hands together close to breastbone (close to the heart center or Charka).

Wear comfortable, loose pants (tights) and top. Cut the feet out of your tights. Your feet are like hands, you need them free. Take care not to have a zipper down the back of your neck. Use an exercise mat or rug that will not slip. Be sure you do not exercise on bare floor. Now, take the phone off the hook, close the door, and give yourself one half hour!

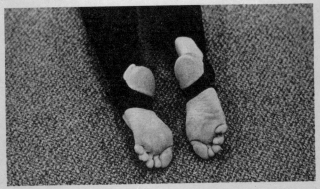

WARNING! None of these exercises are meant to replace the advice of your physician.

Table of Asanas
Asanas recommended for Body-Therapy

Abdomen: All Warmups; Triangle
Asthma: Complete Breath, Fish
Back: Cobra, Locust
Chest: Chest Expander, Cobra, Over Arm Clasp
Chin: (Prevents double chin) Neck Rolls, Lion, Fish
Circulation: Shoulder Stand, Plough, Spinal Twist
Colds: Lion, Shoulder Stand
Constipation: Shoulder Stand, Forward Bend, Yoga
  Mudra
Concentration: Tree, Stork, Bhramari Breath
Energy: Tension Reliever, All Pranayama, Shoulder
  Stand, Sponge
Eye strain: Eye Exercises
Face: Shoulder Stand, Forward Bend, Lion
Fatigue: Tension Reliever, Shoulder Stand, Plough,
  Sponge, Pranayama, Tripod
Female organs: Half Shoulder Stand, Tripod, Fish,
  Plough
Feet (Ankle): Toe Roll, Knee Warmups, Half & Full
  Lotus, Pelvic Posture
Gas pains: Head to Knee Pose, Stomach Lift
Hangover: Plough
Heart: Sponge
High blood pressure: Complete Breath, Alternate
  Breath, Half Shoulder Stand
Low blood pressure: Rock 'n Roll, Cobra, Shoulder,
  Locust, Sun Exercise
Menopause: Cobra, Bow, Locust, Forward Bend
Neck: Neck Roll, Twist
Posture: Cobra, Twist, Easy Posture, Overhand
  Clasp
Relaxation: Tension Reliever, Sun Exercise, Alter-
  nate Breath, Sponge
Round shoulders: Chest Expander, Atlas Posture

Stomach flattener: 2 Leg Raise, Twist, Atlas Posture, Tripod, Churning

Tension: Tension Reliever, All Stretches done with holds, Shoulder Stand, Complete Breath, Alternate Breath, Bhramari Breath

Thyroid problems: Cobra, Shoulder Stand

Throat: Lion, Shoulder Stand

Varicose veins: All inverted Postures

Weight control: Half Shoulder Stand, Full Shoulder Stand, Cobra, Locust and Bow, Spinal Twist, Atlas Posture

Wrists: Anterior Posture, Sun Exercise

Hari Om Tat Sat

Daily Schedule

Beginner (each day)

Tension Reliever
Any 2 leg warmups
Rock N' Roll
Daily Routine
Complete Breath
Deep 10-minute Relaxation

Suggested Practice

Monday	Cow
	Neck Rolls
	Atlas Posture
Tuesday	Knee to Chest
	Forward Bend (hold ½ minute)
	Chest Expander I
Wednesday	Cobra
	Knee Warmups
	½ Lotus
Thursday	The Stork
	Forward Bend
Friday	Cat Stretch
	Locust I
	Folded Leaf
Saturday	½ Shoulder Stand
	Beginner Fish
	Triangle I
Sunday	Bridge I
	Arrow Balance
	Inclined Plane

Intermediate (each day)

Tension Reliever
Any 4 leg warmups
2 or 4 Sun Salutes
Daily Routine
Any 2 Pranayamas
Deep 10-minute Relaxation

Suggested Practice

Monday	Cobra
	Locust I
	Closed Leaf
Tuesday	½ Shoulder Stand
	Fish
	Chest Expansion
Wednesday	Shoulder Stand (hold 3 min.)
	Bridge I
	Knee to Chest
	Forward Bend (hold 1 min.)
Thursday	Forward Bend
	Inclined Plane
	Spinal Twist II
	Pelvic Stretch I
Friday	½ Lotus
	Cobra (3 times)
	Locust II (2 times)
	Bow
Saturday	Rishi Posture
	Eagle
	Triangle
	Shoulder Stand (hold 3 min.)
Sunday	Wood Chopper
	Atlas Posture
	Yoga Mudra
	Plough (hold 2 min.)